# LOCAL COLOR

# LOCAL COLOR

## LONG BEACH ISLAND'S
### HISTORIC PHOTOGRAPHS
### REIMAGINED

**Color** Leslee Ganss  **Words** Ray Fisk

**DOWN THE SHORE**
PUBLISHING
West Creek, New Jersey

Down The Shore Publishing Corp
Box 100, West Creek, N.J. 08092
**www.down-the-shore.com**

The words "Down The Shore" and the Down The Shore Publishing logo are registered U.S. Trademarks.

Printed in China
2 4 6 8 10 9 7 5 3 1

First Printing, 2021

Cover and book design: Leslee Ganss.

Library of Congress Cataloging-in-Publication Data

CIP data was not available at the time this book went to press, but can be found at:
down-the-shore.com/localcolor/cip.html

ISBN 978-1-59322-124-9

# A NAME
# IN THE SAND

Alone I walked the ocean strand
A pearly shell was in my hand
I stopped and wrote upon the sand
My name, the year, the date.
As onward from the spot I passed
One lingering look behind I cast
A wave came rolling high and fast
And washed my lines away.
So shall it be, with every trace on earth of me.
A wave from dark oblivion's sea
Will roll across the place where I have trod
And leave no track or trace.

— *Captain Thomas Bond's favorite poem,*
*by Hanna Flagg Gould.*

*Bond was the proprietor of the Long Beach House,*
*the first major hotel on the Island, predating the Civil*
*War. Located in today's Holgate, it was where, in 1873,*
*Bond was made master of a new U.S. Life-Saving*
*Station that bore his name on the oceanfront.*

Black and white photograph from
*Eighteen Miles of History on Long Beach Island*

# CONTENTS

c. 1960s

# GARVEY,
# LITTLE EGG HARBOR BAY

*This garvey, a traditional bay work boat built
for clamming by local baymen, has been converted
to pleasure boat with a cabin; it is cruising off Beach Haven Gardens.*

*c. 1890*

## SEA COTTAGE, LONG BEACH ISLAND

Black and white photograph from
*Island Album*

# INTRODUCTION

A picture is worth a thousand words, the old adage goes.

But what happens when photographs are so commonplace that they lose their meaning and their value is just another click? What happens when images become background noise? In this age when we're drowning in images and media, and apps can make every cellphone photo appear interesting, how do we find authenticity?

As a publisher who has worked with historic images for nearly four decades, that's the challenge we're trying to meet with this book. The Long Beach Island photographs published here reveal lives and moments from a world that no longer exists. How do we transport ourselves back into those lives and moments? How do we get to a place where we can actually *feel* that world?

In our earlier books about Island history, old pictures were only starting to emerge in public from yellowing albums and dusty attics; they hadn't been widely shared beyond family and neighbors. Readers would pore over those pages, absorbing stories and imagining — through never-before-seen photos — a younger Island.

The digital world has altered our perceptions about images. We're a bit jaded. We see a steady stream of photos — online, in messages, Facebook groups, Instagram, and other social media. All too frequently they're presented without context — without the story that could enlighten us. At times inaccurate history is attached to old photos. Historic images are also employed to persuade, to sell, to convince us that a business or product has deep roots and is connected to our shared past. Sadly, the visual content becomes devalued.

We wanted to break free of that; to find a way to present our history with new vibrance, yet still give a soulful and honest sense of place. To make it easily discovered despite our limited attention. To breathe new life into historic photos even if we've seen them elsewhere. We wanted to do this with an integrity that respects the original image and respects the people captured in that image — to show the humanity of this place.

In *Local Color*, carefully selected historic photographs have been hand-colored; we present them with brief descriptions, short excerpts or quotes distilled from decades of publishing local history. The authors of these passages and those they quote give context and hopefully enhance the feeling evoked by the photograph.

The photographs and words are presented as if in a gallery, so readers can linger on a scene, one at a time. The chronology is roughly by decade, somewhat overlapping, encompassing a little over a century from the late 1870s to the early 1980s.

This was an era of black and white film, and the original photographs in this book were all made on film or glass plates. We've added color — by hand, mostly on a computer — making very human and deliberate decisions about every detail. Decisions about elements like color, shading or hue are based on experiences living here, immersed in the Shore and its history. It's an honest and informed hand-coloring, not performed by an algorithm or app, a process that took place over several years.

In selecting the images, we were constantly drawn to scenes that revealed daily activities without pretense — the seashore jobs and working life, the silly and frivolous, the summer fun. Landmarks like lighthouses and the old hotels are here, along with vanished wetlands, wild beaches, and the aftermath of coastal storms. The images are mostly casual, everyday photographs, the kind you find in family albums. We've included many of the earliest photographs used to promote the new Island communities, some by Robert F. Engle, a professional trained at the turn of the last century who was son of the founder of the Engleside Hotel. Others, from mid-century, are by the prolific Bill Kane, who sold them at his shop, the Nor'easter in Beach Haven Terrace. The photographers are no longer with us, but we're fortunate to have their work, a monochrome legacy that documents Long Beach Island's past.

It was a delight to work with the original prints and find handwritten notes in pencil or old quill ink, often on the back. These clues allowed us to discern a more accurate story from the image. We looked for a date, or names, a location, a memory or description — anything that might add to an understanding of the world and the aura of that time.

Many photographs included have appeared, black and white, in our other titles. Those books are referenced in each credit so readers can refer to them for a fuller history. In many cases, there may be an entire chapter about the subject, such as rumrunning, the railroad, or pound fishing. Because different books have different or additional historical details, at times we've paired a photograph from one title with a short excerpt or quote from another.

The timeframe here — when most photographs were black and white, when photography was not so easy and commonplace — is also a time when individual photographs were treasured. It's an era that aligns with the founding of Beach Haven as a summer resort and a century of growth and change on Long Beach Island.

We hope you can appreciate these photographs as if they were just found in one of those yellowing albums in a dusty attic, but with new life animating them, and your connection to Long Beach Island is even more full.

— *Ray Fisk*

*1955*

## LIFEJACKET
## ON THE BEACH,
## BEACH HAVEN

Black and white photograph by
Rodney Connor, from *Island Album*

# LONG BEACH ISLAND'S
## HISTORIC PHOTOGRAPHS
### REIMAGINED

## SALT HAY HARVEST
## ON A SCOW

Spartina patens, *the verdant salt grass of the tidal marshlands, was harvested by hand and later using horse- and ox-drawn teams along Barnegat and Little Egg Harbor bays. Resistant to mold, it was used into the early 1900s in everything from commercial packing for glassware, pottery, and even bananas, to livestock feed and mattresses.*

Black and white photograph from
*Two Centuries of History on Long Beach Island*

15

*early 1900s*

## BRIDGE TENDER'S HOUSE AND TRESTLE, LOOKING EAST FROM THE MANAHAWKIN MEADOWS

*"We clickety-clacked through miles of scrub growth and at last saw Barnegat Bay and inhaled the salty smell of the meadows. The trip across the bay trestle seemed endless and I recall looking at the water on either side and wondering where I was going."*

— *Muriel Oliver Tooker, in* Island Album

Black and white photograph from
*Eighteen Miles of History on Long Beach Island*

*c. 1880*

# ASHLEY HOUSE
# AND BARNEGAT LIGHTHOUSE

*The north end of Long Beach Island was part of the estate
of John M. Brown, a former wreckmaster, who purchased
large parcels of land on both sides of the inlet in 1855. The
properties included this boardinghouse known as the Herring
House, built in 1821. Brown enlarged and rebuilt it, renaming
it after his mother Ashley. The final owner of the one-time
whitewashed, sprawling hostelry was J. Warner Kinsey, who left
to manage the new Sunset Hotel in 1884. The north end of the
Island became known as Barnegat City by 1881 and in 1948
formally changed its name to Barnegat Light.*

Black and white photograph: Ocean County Historical Society;
from *Long Beach Island Chronicles.*

*late 1800s*

# LIFE-SAVING SERVICE DRILL, BOND'S STATION

*On Long Beach Island, there were five U.S. Life-Saving stations, plus one on Tucker's Island. It was common to see life-saving crews practice with equipment all along the Shore in the early part of the century. Crewmen like these men from Bond's station in Holgate would have to pull a lifeboat through soft sand to the location of a wreck, often more than a mile from the station.*

Black and white photograph from
*Six Miles At Sea*

# LITTLE EGG HARBOR LIGHT, TUCKER'S ISLAND

*Also known as Tucker's Light and Tucker Beach Lighthouse, the beacon on Tucker's Island, six miles south of Beach Haven, was built on ground subject to the whims of coastal geography. The long spit of beach south of Beach Haven (the Holgate Unit of the Edwin B. Forsythe National Wildlife Refuge today), had variously been a beach and a separate island. There was even a small year-round community called Sea Haven that was lost to the tides. In October of 1927, the lighthouse itself fell into the sea. Here, a two-masted schooner can be seen heading out Little Egg Harbor Inlet beyond the beach.*

Black and white photograph from
*Eighteen Miles of History on Long Beach Island*

*c. 1870s -1880s*

## PADDLE-WHEEL STEAMBOAT *POHATCONG*, EDGE COVE, TUCKERTON

*After the construction of the Tuckerton Railroad in 1872, a spur track was built to Edge Cove in the marshlands, where steamboats and sailboats ferried passengers to Bond's Long Beach House and the Parry House at the southern end of the Island. The Pohatcong was one of three steamers that operated for a dozen years from Tuckerton. At the north end of the Island, two steamboats ran from the south shore of the Toms River and Barnegat.*

Black and white photograph from
*Eighteen Miles of History on Long Beach Island*

*c. 1890s*

## DOCK ROAD, BEACH HAVEN

*The first entrance to Beach Haven was Mud Hen Creek and later Dock Road alongside the creek. Before the railroad in 1886, all building materials for the young resort town arrived by sailboat from the mainland, and visitors came by sailboat and steamboat. The creek and the wetlands were eventually filled in and the original cedar log corduroy road was improved to the fine condition seen in this photograph. The Hotel DeCrab is at left, and at the end of the road is the Beach Haven House. In the far distance, to the left of the original wooden water tower, is the tower of the Engleside Hotel on the beach.*

Black and white photograph:
Lloyd family collection

*c. 1870s*

## HOTEL DECRAB, BEACH HAVEN

*Towed on a barge from Harvey Cedars in 1873, this decommissioned government "house of refuge" for shipwreck survivors was relocated over Mud Hen Creek alongside Dock Road in Beach Haven. For nearly a decade it was the only permanent structure on Dock Road. Proprietor Captain John Tilton Fox served boat captains carrying building materials and ferrying passengers to the new resort town.*

Black and white photograph:
Lloyd family collection

*mid-1890s*

## KEEPER'S HOUSE AND BARNEGAT LIGHTHOUSE

*The U.S. Lighthouse Board built in 1859, and expanded in 1893, a huge, two-and-one-half-story frame dwelling at the base of the light for the keepers and three families. Decades later, erosion from storms was so severe that the structure was sold for scrap; by May of 1920 the entire house had been demolished.*

*"It was all one building, but it was partitioned so that each family had separate quarters. The big keeper's house with its multiple brick chimneys became, in time, as familiar a landmark as the light itself. Around the keeper's house was a picturesque grove of trees, all that remained of several acres of woods long since washed away. Within this grove was a narrow, shaded trail leading from the keeper's house to the edge of the sea. It never failed to enchant visitors. This trail, were it not now under water, would today be East 2nd Street in Barnegat Light."*

— *John Bailey Lloyd, in* Six Miles At Sea

Black and white photograph by Minnie D. Kelly:
Barnegat Light Museum

*c. 1890s*

# ENGLESIDE HOTEL, BEACH HAVEN

*Distinguished by its tower, the Engleside — built in just six months in 1876, the year of America's centennial — was one of two big oceanfront hotels in the young resort of Beach Haven.*

*"The tower never contained anything but four levels of breezy porches full of wicker rockers, but it was a most charming place to be. On clear summer days in the 1890s it was not uncommon to see 100 to 150 fore and aft-rigged sailing craft off Long Beach Island and a continual parade of small coasters. The big tower's outward appearance gave the building a grace and majesty beyond compare."*

*— John Bailey Lloyd,*
*in* Eighteen Miles of History on Long Beach Island

Black and white photograph from
*Eighteen Miles of History on Long Beach Island*

33

*c. 1890*

## BEACH HAVEN TERRACE
## TRAIN STATION

*Early real estate developments on the Island were often
marketed near stops on the Manahawkin and Long
Beach Railroad, but the nearby Long Beach Life-Saving Station
was the nucleus of a new resort called
Beach Haven Terrace in 1907.*

Black and white photograph from
*Island Album*

c. *1890*

# ANGLERS AND CREW OF THE *OWL*
# WITH A WEAKFISH CATCH
# AT THE WHARF, BEACH HAVEN

*"In the last three decades of the 19th century, saltwater
fishing drew more visitors to the Shore than any other sport
except gunning.... So abundant were the weakfish, croakers,
sheepshead and flounder that one person could catch more
fish in two hours than could possibly be eaten in a month.
Most of these catches went to waste for lack of refrigeration
and many a big fish could have been tossed back to bite
again, but no one, much less the captain himself, wanted to
return to the dock empty-handed. An overflowing fish box
was the surest sign of a good trip, the very best
way to stimulate future business."*

— *John Bailey Lloyd in*
Eighteen Miles of History on Long Beach Island.

Black and white photograph by Robert F. Engle,
from *Eighteen Miles of History on Long Beach Island.* Lloyd family collection.

*c. 1880s*

## LITTLE EGG HARBOR LIGHTHOUSE (TUCKER'S LIGHT), TUCKER'S ISLAND

*In 1879, the federal Lighthouse Board completed the final improvements to the lighthouse on Tucker's Island, and this photograph may have been made around that time as it shows the structure in its prime — possibly with some of Lighthouse Keeper Eber Rider's family posing on the porch. The keeper's house has been enlarged with a second floor and a black light tower above. The original 1848 Tucker's Beach light is at left — the 40-foot tower shortened and used for oil storage. The original light had been abandoned during the Civil War, then relit in 1867 with the addition of the smaller keeper's house.*

Black and white photograph from
*Six Miles At Sea*

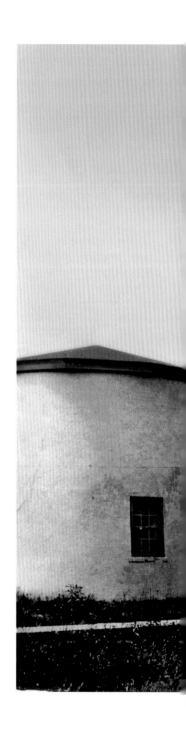

*c. 1890s*

## SARA AND EARL McCONNELL, HOLGATE

Black and white photograph from an
original print: Lloyd family collection

41

# THE BUNGALOW ON WOOD'S ISLAND, OFF HARVEY CEDARS

*Built in 1892 as a vacation home on an island in Barnegat Bay, the cottage was converted in 1903 into a hunting club. It was accessible by a footbridge from the Passaic Avenue train stop in Harvey Cedars. For the next two decades, a circle of politically influential Pennsylvania friends of owner William Henry Sayen enjoyed fishing, gunning and card playing at the cottage, calling themselves the "Bold Buccaneers of the Bungalow." One member, Robert W. A. Wood, a Pennsylvania wool merchant, bought it in 1920 for his family. Often referred to as the Harvey Cedars Gunning Club (and in Bayard Kraft's book, Under Barnegat's Beam, as the Harvey Cedars Outing Club), to the Wood family it was always the bungalow. In the early years they sometimes called it the "House of the Seven Cedars" for the few gnarled trees remaining on the little island. A fire in 1933 destroyed the home, and today even the island has eroded away and only weathered cedar pilings remain visible at low tide.*

Black and white photograph from
*Two Centuries of History on Long Beach Island*

*c. 1898*

## ON A CATBOAT, WEST CREEK

*"Newbie McConnell. Taken up
West Creek, N.J. about 1898"*

*— note on the back of this photograph.*

Black and white photograph from an original print:
Lloyd family collection.

*c. 1903*

## SHIP BOTTOM
## LIFE-SAVING STATIONS

*Children play in sandy lots by the new U.S. Life-Saving Station, built in 1898, on the left, and the original 1872 station, on the right. The original station is still standing on Ship Bottom Avenue and is a private home. The Life-Saving Service became the Coast Guard in 1915.*

Black and white photograph from
*Island Album*

*early 1900s*

## SEAWEED GATHERERS NORTH OF BARNEGAT LIGHTHOUSE

*By 1920 the dunes had been eroded by storms and the keeper's house at the foot of the lighthouse was so imperiled it was abandoned by the Bureau of Lighthouses. It was sold for its scrap value that year. Today this area is part of Barnegat Inlet.*

Black and white photograph from
*Island Album*

49

# CATBOATS ON
# LITTLE EGG HARBOR BAY

*Before the railroad connected Long Beach Island to the mainland in 1886, the only transportation across the bay was a boat, primarily sail, although steamboats operated from 1872 until the railroad was completed. Visitors to the new hotels in Beach Haven and Barnegat City — as well as all building materials and provisions — traveled on the water from Tuckerton, West Creek and Barnegat. Professional captains were in constant demand and formed the Beach Haven Yacht Club to coordinate activities. They held frequent races in the late 1800s. Scenes of the broad, beamy catboats, with their gaff-rigged sails — a shallow-draft design in perfect harmony with the environment — added an element of grace and beauty to the bay.*

Black and white photograph from
*Six Miles At Sea*

*c. early 1900s*

## CORINTHIAN YACHT AND GUN CLUB, BEACH HAVEN

*Built in 1904 at the corner of Marine Street and Beach Avenue for the Beach Haven Gun Club, the group soon enlarged the building and changed its name to provide "for the needs of the growing number of amateur boatmen whose interests were not being well served by the better-established Beach Haven Yacht Club." John Bailey Lloyd characterized the membership of 30 summer residents as "unabashedly aristocratic in tone" but, unlike other clubs, women were welcome and joined the men in trap shooting and bird hunting. Note on the photograph describes this gathering as "afternoon tea." The membership was absorbed into the Little Egg Harbor Yacht Club in 1912. The house was demolished in 1984 to make way for two duplexes on the lot.*

Black and white photograph from
*Eighteen Miles of History on Long Beach Island*

*c. 1900*

## REMAINS OF BOND'S
## LONG BEACH HOUSE, HOLGATE

*From 1851 until 1883, Captain Thomas Bond operated the
first hotel on Long Beach Island, known since the 1820s as the
Philadelphia Company House. Catering mostly to sportsmen,
guests would arrive by sailboat. "Of the eight major hotels
built on Long Beach Island before the coming of the railroad
in 1886... the most significant of these was the famous Long
Beach House of Thomas Bond. Out of it and the
influential men who stayed there over the years
came the genesis of Beach Haven."*

— *John Bailey Lloyd,
in* Eighteen Miles of History on Long Beach Island

Black and white photograph from
*Eighteen Miles of History on Long Beach Island*

c. *1900*

## SAILING IN A CATBOAT, LITTLE EGG HARBOR BAY

Black and white photograph:
Lloyd family collection

c. 1905

## THE BEACH AT
## BEACH HAVEN

*A wooden walkway leads to the
beach from the boardwalk.*

Black and white photograph from
*Eighteen Miles of History on Long Beach Island*

# SEA HAVEN SCHOOLHOUSE, TUCKER'S ISLAND

*Students and their teacher, Florence Morss, pose outside their one-room schoolhouse in the waning days of their little community on Tucker's Island. Also known as St. Albans-by-the-Sea, Sea Haven was created in 1879 with the hope that it would compete with the success of Beach Haven, five miles to the north. The community included this 1895 schoolhouse — funded by clambakes — two hotels, a life-saving station, and the Little Egg Harbor Lighthouse. By the late 1940s, storms and erosion had washed away most of Tucker's Beach and Island; the schoolhouse was the last building to vanish into the sea.*

Black and white photograph from Barbara L. Windrow,
in *Eighteen Miles of History on Long Beach Island*

*c. 1900*

## BEACH GAMES, ENGLESIDE HOTEL, BEACH HAVEN

*This potato-on-a-spoon race was one of a constant round of activities for guests of the hotel.*

Black and white photograph from a glass negative by Robert F. Engle; from *Eighteen Miles of History on Long Beach Island*

*c. 1898*

## SAILING ON A CATBOAT, LITTLE EGG HARBOR BAY

*Related photographs with brief handwritten notes on the back tell us this was a sailing excursion of the McConnell family from the Beck Farm, off Liberty Avenue in Beach Haven, across the bay and up the Westecunk Creek in West Creek.*

Black and white photograph from an original print:
Lloyd family collection

*c. 1905*

# POUND FISHING CREW, HARVEY CEDARS

*The crew of Isaac Lee's pound fishery pose with a horse team. The Sea Gull house was on the northeast corner of 76th Street and today's Boulevard until the middle of the century.*

Black and white photograph:
Collection of Margaret Thomas Buchholz

*1907*

## HARVEY CEDARS HOTEL

*Captain Samuel Perrine bought the Connahassatt House in 1841 and expanded it into the Harvey Cedars Hotel in 1848. In 1903 a gas lighting system was installed. Of the eight large 19th-century hotels on the Island, it is the only one standing today. The Philadelphia YWCA purchased the property in the early 1930s and operated Camp Whelan there. Today it is the Harvey Cedars Bible Conference, a Christian retreat.*

Black and white photograph from
*Island Album*

## 1903

# ENGLESIDE HOTEL GUESTS ON THE BEACH, BEACH HAVEN

*Outfitted for a musical skit, Engleside guests clown on the beach for photographer Robert F. Engle, son of the hotel's founder. The Engles organized dances, concerts, games, minstrel shows, costume parties and other activities at their Beach Haven hotel to keep everyone constantly entertained. The son was a serious photographer, working with the most famous travel lecturer of his day and traveling throughout the nation, Mexico, and Europe.*

Glass negative photograph by Robert F. Engle: from *Eighteen Miles of History on Long Beach Island*

# CREW AT THE SHIP BOTTOM LIFE-SAVING STATION

*Five life-saving stations were established on Long Beach Island near the oceanfront dunes at Barnegat Inlet, Loveladies, Harvey Cedars, Ship Bottom, Beach Haven Terrace and Holgate. Bond's, the Holgate station, was the location of one of the original houses of refuge since 1850. The Little Egg Station on Tucker's Island was two miles south of Bond's. This crew at Ship Bottom is, from left: A. Brad Simmons, "Long John" Cranmer, Jim Henry Cranmer, Bart Pharo, J. Horace Cranmer, Caleb Conklin, Captain "Ike" Truex, and the dog, Tippy.*

Black and white photograph from
*Six Miles At Sea*

*July 1909*

## TRAIN PASSES THROUGH
## HARVEY CEDARS

*The Manahawkin and Long Beach Railroad began operations with its first route to Barnegat City in June 1886 and a month later to Beach Haven. Passenger service peaked in 1920. Trains stopped running to the north end of the Island in 1923. Service to Beach Haven was freight only after 1930 and all operations ceased in November 1935 when the trestle over the bay was destroyed in a northeast storm. In the 49 years of the railroad on the Island, the parent Pennsylvania Railroad lost more than a million dollars.*

Black and white photograph from
*Six Miles At Sea*

K. Watts
July 1909

c. 1916

# BARNEGAT INLET

*In a few years storms and erosion would bring about
the demise of the impressive keeper's house at the foot of
Barnegat Lighthouse, but here a pleasure boat anchors in the
inlet as strollers walk the sandy edge. Small vessels
were still largely powered by wind, so this craft,
with an inboard engine, towing a dinghy,
must have been a novelty.*

Black and white photograph by Lewis D. Crowell;
from an original print: Lloyd family collection

*c. 1910*

## ENGLESIDE HOTEL BEACH, BEACH HAVEN

*Before Island towns organized paid beach patrols, the two big hotels provided a guarded beach for their guests. In this image, primitive lifesaving equipment — a backboard and a spooled rescue line — can be seen at the edge of the water. A guard can be seen rowing at right beyond the breakers.*

Black and white photograph from
*Six Miles At Sea*

*c. 1910*

## JOSEPHINE THE BEAR, BEACH HAVEN

*Josephine and his owner came by train for two weeks every summer. For dinner they would go to the Ocean House bar and as night would fall they went to the boardwalk and slept underneath the boards. The bear got a bucket full of beer that eventually made him sleepy.*

Black and white photograph:
Lloyd family collection

*January 1910*

## BEACHGOERS POSE ON THE HULL OF THE *FORTUNA*, SHIP BOTTOM-BEACH ARLINGTON

*The steel-hulled Italian bark Fortuna, bound for New York from Barbados, ran aground in heavy fog at 16th Street in today's Ship Bottom. But it was an earlier shipwreck in March of 1817 that gave the town its name. In that tragedy, a young woman was the only survivor after rescuers chopped a hole in the overturned ship's bottom near the keel to pull her to safety.*

Black and white photograph from
*Six Miles At Sea*

c. 1910

## TUG-OF-WAR,
## BEACH HAVEN

Black and white photograph:
collection of the New Jersey Maritime Museum

# BEACH HAVEN TERRACE
# POST OFFICE AND STORE

*This building, better known in later years as the Nor'easter store, operated by Bill Kane, is shown a year before the automobile causeway opened and the Terrace was a stop on the railroad. Until the early '20s, the train was still the primary means of transportation for most potential buyers of Shore homes, and Philadelphia realtors ran Saturday morning excursion trains to the Island. The nucleus of Beach Haven Terrace, however, was Life-Saving Station 117, the Long Beach Station, which still stands as a private home today.*

Black and white photograph:
Lloyd family collection

*c. 1915*

# GUNNING PARTY, LITTLE EGG HARBOR BAY

*New Jersey Governor Walter E. Edge is on the right in this group on a marsh island in the bay. He was a frequent guest of Charles Beck at "The Farm," the Beck estate in Beach Haven. Since the late 1800s duck hunting attracted wealthy, ambitious men, like Jay Cooke, a major financier of the Union Army and American railroads; they were often guests at the Engleside Hotel.*

*"By the opening of the 20th-century the blast of guns that began at sunrise seldom ended until late in the day. Gunning was so good in the spring of 1901 that it was a common sight to see hunters in the streets of Tuckerton with wheelbarrow loads of freshly killed waterfowl. One Saturday night in April, 1901, 800 brant to be shipped to Philadelphia were counted. Most gunners were getting 50 or 60 birds per man a day, mostly brant, which panicked and tended to bunch together, offering an easy target. One party of three bagged 108 broadbill near the Crab Island fish factory."*
— *John Bailey Lloyd, in* Six Miles At Sea

Black and white photograph: collection
of the New Jersey Maritime Museum

*1919*

# CHILDREN PLAY ON
# ERODED BEACH,
# BARNEGAT CITY

*As storms and erosion threatened Barnegat Lighthouse and the keeper's house, the first efforts to build a riprap groin — a jetty — were underway. But the keeper's house was doomed; storms the following winter forced the federal Bureau of Lighthouses to abandon efforts to save it. An earlier concrete bulkhead in front of the house had already partially collapsed in the center and is rubble in this photograph. Sailing fishing vessels off the inlet can be seen in the far right on the horizon.*

Black and white photograph: Barnegat Light Museum; from *Eighteen Miles of History on Long Beach Island*

1914-1959

# CAUSEWAY DRAWBRIDGE

*Traffic on the original wooden plank causeway was halted whenever a boat in the channel between Cedar Bonnet Island and Ship Bottom was passing and the drawbridge was opened.*

*"The old causeway is the one common link in the collective memories of those who can remember the island of the 1950s and earlier. The rumble of the boards, that first whiff of salt air, that thin line of lights across the water after dark, the broken clams dropped by sea gulls, the whitecaps level with the road in a northeaster are all images and sensations shared by motorists to Long Beach Island for 45 years, from 1914 until 1959."*

— *John Bailey Lloyd in* Eighteen Miles of History on Long Beach Island

Black and white photograph from
*Six Miles At Sea*

92

Bathing Bea

*1919*

## SURF CITY

*Girls pose for a beach photograph
in front of Victorian oceanfronts.*

Black and white photograph from
*Six Miles At Sea*

*1919*

# BEACH EROSION,
# BARNEGAT LIGHT

*"The Melhorn's two story Victorian house, built on a sturdy brick foundation, was the next to go.... The foundation under the porch and front rooms was completely washed away, and the structure stood, still erect, but precariously on the edge of a sand dune.... One Saturday in April or May of 1919, I was working on cleaning the wick of the kerosene stove... There were shouts of people and Papa pointed. 'The Melhorn's place, it's going over!' I grabbed a box camera from the old mission table and ran down the beach. From two blocks distant, I could hear the screeching, rending, bedlam of moving beams and heavy timbers many years unmolested.... The house fell heavily onto its side on the beach. There was a deep rumble of furniture thundering across the rooms. The destruction, which seemed to take an eternity, was actually over in less than a minute. As the tide closed in, it was under an hour until the debris hardly resembled the remains of a house at all."*

— *Barnegat City Mayor T. J. France, in his book,* The Decline and Fall of the Oceanic Hotel and Tales of the Barnegat Lighthouse

Black and white photograph by T. J. France:
Barnegat Light Museum

*c. 1919*

## CONSTRUCTING AN EARLY JETTY NEAR BARNEGAT LIGHTHOUSE

*The first small rock groins on Long Beach Island were constructed to protect Barnegat Lighthouse and the keeper's house from severe erosion. Riprap was used and gondola cars on the train brought 50-ton boulders to Barnegat City; teams of horses delivered them to the beach. It was not until 1939, however, that construction began on a full jetty on the north side of the inlet.*

Black and white photograph from an original print:
Lloyd family collection

*c. 1920*

## A TRAIN LEAVES THE BEACH HAVEN STATION

*"On that long-ago summer morning when the first engine of the Long Beach Railroad chuffed triumphantly into Beach Haven, the hotels emptied to celebrate the occasion. The scream of the engine's whistle, its clanging bell and hissing clouds of steam answered by the cheering crowds ushered in a new era of swift, comfortable trips to the seashore. But there was another effect. July 24, 1886 marked the beginning of a change in the physical appearance of the island. Long Beach Island was still a wild and beautifully desolate stretch of bogs, bushes and sand dunes...."*

— John Bailey Lloyd, in Eighteen Miles of History on Long Beach Island

Black and white photograph from
*Six Miles At Sea*

# A LOAD OF EELGRASS,
# HARVEY CEDARS

*Charles Smedley atop a wagonload of eelgrass, the
"seaweed" of the bay. At right is Kinsey's General Store, on
the northeast corner of 78th Street. "The Kinsey Seamoss
Company sold its product as an inexpensive mattress
stuffing to prisons and steamship lines. It was in demand
for cheap upholstery, including the seats of Model T Fords,
and for insulating buildings.... The United Fruit Company
bought seaweed for packing and shipping bananas.... In the
early 1900s, hardly a family in this area did not have some
connection with the seaweed business."*

— *Dorothy Thomas, in* The Long Beach Island Reader

Black and white photograph from
*Island Album*

c. 1920s

# BEACH HAVEN OCEANFRONT AND ENGLESIDE HOTEL

*Natural dunes and a sparsely developed beachfront are evident inside the boardwalk in this view, looking south and west from about 2nd Street. Sand traps, coarse grass and water hazards offered the right terrain for Engleside Hotel guests to play beach golf — a new fad in the 1920s.*

Black and white photograph from
*Six Miles At Sea*

*1925*

## "DAD,"
## BARNEGAT CITY BEACH

*"Joseph A. Letts formerly of Camden and Waretown,
N.J. Father of Evelyn C. Brown, Parkertown, N.J."
— note on back of the original photograph.*

Black and white photograph from an original print:
Lloyd family collection

Dad

*1922*

# PIE-EATING CONTEST, BEACH HAVEN

*The one and only Ocean County Day, July 15, 1922, included tug-of-war, plus wheelbarrow and three-legged races on the beach, as well as a pie-eating contest. Swimming events were held at the Little Egg Harbor Yacht Club, and races with college athletes on the graveled street in front of the Engleside Hotel. Organized by boosters of Beach Haven, the event was held at the Engleside and attracted a thousand people on the boardwalk. Hundreds arrived on excursion trains from Philadelphia; others motored across the causeway bridge from other parts of the county.*

Black and white photograph from
*Two Centuries of History on Long Beach Island*

*1920*

## VIEW FROM THE OCEANIC HOTEL, BARNEGAT CITY

*The Oceanic Hotel was undergoing demolition because of the severe beach erosion washing away Barnegat City's oceanfront when this photograph was made, October 22, 1920. The majestic Barnegat Lighthouse keeper's house, seen in the distance, was also being disassembled and sold for scrap, as the ocean undercut its foundation. The boxcar, seemingly on a track to the sea, had been parked at the northern terminus of the railroad near the hotel's platform.*

Black and white photograph: Barnegat Light Museum; from *Long Beach Island Chronicles*

*c. 1920*

# POUND FISHING SKIFF PULLED ONSHORE BY TEAM OF HORSES, LONG BEACH ISLAND

*Pound fishing on the Island began after railroad service was established in 1886, allowing for the transport of a catch to city markets.*

*"The industry was most active on Long Beach Island in the 1920s and 1930s, when there were five major pound fisheries in operation. Beach Haven had the Sun Fishery and the Beach Haven Fishery. A few miles to the north there was Tonnes Bohn's Crest Fishery, and in Ship Bottom, across the road from each other at the entrance to the island, the Barnegat City Fishery and the Surf City Fishery, which had moved there in 1923 when train service was discontinued on the north end of the island. Each of these five companies owned and maintained at least four or five pound net installations out in the ocean, working them from April through November."*

— *John Bailey Lloyd, in*
Eighteen Miles of History on Long Beach Island

Black and white photograph:
Lloyd family collection

c. 1920

# TRAIN APPROACHING BAY TRESTLE, MANAHAWKIN MEADOWS

*With the powerful Pennsylvania Railroad as its parent, the Manahawkin and Long Beach Railroad began operations to both ends of Long Beach Island in 1886. It was managed by the local Tuckerton Railroad which first delivered passengers to the Island, by way of the Edge Cove boat landing in Tuckerton, in 1872. A northeast storm on November 17, 1935 destroyed a mile of trestle and resulted in the end of railroad service on the Island.*

Black and white photograph from
*Eighteen Miles of History on Long Beach Island*

c. *1920*

# BEACH HAVEN
# BASEBALL CLUB

*A 1920s Beach Haven team that won 40 out of 49 games: Left to right, first row: Lud Wray, Clarence (Tuck) Parker, Chris Sprague, "Weary" Walker, Edward Sprague; second row: Charles Cramer, Yeomon Penrod, George "Tip" Barclay, A. Paul King, Alec Wray.*

*"In the 1880s and 1890s there was scarcely a small town in America that did not have its own baseball team ready to take on any other team within fifty miles. Young men wore their baggy woolen uniforms and round, visored caps with pride. The whole community turned out to cheer them. They were true heroes who aspired to play in the majors, and some of them, like Roger 'Doc' Cramer of Beach Haven, were spotted and actually made it."*

*— John Bailey Lloyd, in Six Miles At Sea.*

Black and white photograph from
*Two Centuries of History on Long Beach Island*

This team won 40 out of 49 games, only three teams collected over three hits, those of the nine games lost was extra innings { one 18 inning 1-0 " 13 " 3-0 " 12 " 2-1

*c. 1920*

## ENGLESIDE HOTEL BEACH, BEACH HAVEN

Black and white photograph from
*Eighteen Miles of History on Long Beach Island*

*c. 1920s*

## JAPANESE NOVELTY STORE, BOARDWALK, BEACH HAVEN

*"The first store on the new boardwalk in 1920 was the Japanese Novelty Shop of Haidee Nakamura, who leased space in the east end of the Baldwin bathhouses at Marine Street. Nakamura sold fancy wares of silk and bamboo, little dolls with porcelain heads, incense, wind chimes and firecrackers. It was only here that one could buy the handsome glazed chinaware hand-painted with images of Beach Haven landmarks, sets so eagerly sought by collectors today."*

— *John Bailey Lloyd, in*
Eighteen Miles of History on Long Beach Island

Black and white photograph from
*Eighteen Miles of History on Long Beach Island*

*c. 1920s*

## BALDWIN HOTEL AND BOARDWALK, BEACH HAVEN

*With its distinctive minarets, the New Hotel Baldwin was one of two grand oceanfront hotels in the booming resort of Beach Haven. The mile-long boardwalk, built in 1917, was destroyed in a September 1944 hurricane that devastated much of Long Beach Island and was never rebuilt. The Baldwin burned to the ground in a spectacular fire driven by gale-force winds on September 24, 1960.*

Black and white photograph from
*Eighteen Miles of History on Long Beach Island*

# BARNEGAT LIGHTHOUSE KEEPER'S FAMILY

*The second, and current, Barnegat Lighthouse was built between 1856 and 1859, but the grand two-and-one-half story keeper's house was not constructed until 1889. During the winter of 1919-1920, severe storms washed away entire streets in Barnegat City and homes were either moved or fell into the sea. To the dismay of residents, the U.S. Bureau of Lighthouses determined that the erosion was so bad that the threatened keeper's house could not be saved. It was sold for scrap for $120. Here a keeper's family poses amid erosion debris at the side of the house, capturing a last moment before the house, and the era of keepers, is gone.*

Black and white photograph:
Lloyd family collection.

*c. 1920*

# POUND FISHERMEN
# AND BOATS ON
# THE BEACH

*"There were seven, sometimes eight men in a pound boat.
We rolled them down to the surf, we had to pull way out,
about a thousand foot offshore, and we all pulled on that line.
Sometimes the weather would be bad and we'd have to bail it
out, and try again until we made it and cleared the sand. We
had a one-cylinder Hartford engine, can't figure out how they
got away with the noise it made — like cannon shots every
time that thing fired. The nets were about two or three miles
out; the inshore poles were about 35 feet long, the offshore
ones about 80 feet. The fish would follow a long, straight row
of poles lined with nets until they got trapped in the square
pocket in the middle. Then we'd go out there and pull the
nets up by hand, part of the net, and scoop the fish out. It
might take three or four hours; sometimes we got four or five
hundred barrels. That would be a big day.
The price of fish was very low."*

— *Paul Gundersen, in* Island Album

Black and white photograph from *Island Album*

*1927*

# IMPERILED
# LITTLE EGG HARBOR LIGHT,
# TUCKER'S ISLAND

*Lighthouse Keeper Arthur H. T. Rider made the following report to his superiors at the Third District office after a severe northeast storm on the 20th of February 1927: "Nearly all of the foundation was washed away from the front of the building. The old hotel (the St. Alban's) that stood about 200 feet away and another house 500 feet away were washed down and totally destroyed." The Bureau of Lighthouses discontinued the light station on September 30, and on October 12 the lighthouse was washed into the sea.*

Black and white photograph from
*Eighteen Miles of History on Long Beach Island*

# BALES OF EELGRASS, HARVEY CEDARS

*"I bounced from one thing to the other after I was mustered out of the Marines. In the early 1920s, I came down to the Island where I'd spent summers as a boy and went to work for J.B. Kinsey, my mother's brother. He had a seaweed business, the Kinsey Sea Moss Company. We gathered the grass up from the bay where it floated in huge windrows, shifting with the tide and wind. If the wind was from the east, we gathered it in barges; but if the wind was from the west, it did the job for us, washing it up onto the meadows. It was green and slimy, we used pitchforks to spread it over the stubby meadow grass where the rain cleaned it, and then we left it out to dry for several weeks. My uncle owned the whole Harvey Cedars bayfront north of 80th Street and that was his drying ground. After it dried it was pressed into bales. We shipped the bales out on the railroad; there couldn't have been a business without the trains. Our major customer was United Fruit Company. They bought the stuff by the carloads, used it for packing fruit. Other companies used it for upholstery, padding coffins and cheap mattresses made by prisoners. As it was fireproof, the eelgrass was used as insulation on some Island homes."*

— *Reynold Thomas, in* Island Album

Black and white photograph from
*Island Album*

*c. 1920s*

## ENGLESIDE HOTEL STAFF RINSE THEIR HAIR IN RAINWATER, BEACH HAVEN

*"Nearly all of the waitresses at the Engleside came from Boston, where Engle advertised for help. Their good looks, humor and lilting Irish accents were as much a part of dining there as the clatter of heavy china and silver. Most of them were still in school, some in college, usually living at home with their parents in the winter months, so they welcomed this chance to get away, and many came back year after year. They lived in a three-story building on the northeast corner of Beach Avenue and Amber Street, and they dated the local boys when they went out at night."*

— *John Bailey Lloyd,*
*in* Eighteen Miles of History on Long Beach Island

Black and white photograph from
*Eighteen Miles of History on Long Beach Island*

*October 12, 1927*

# LITTLE EGG HARBOR LIGHTHOUSE FALLS INTO THE SEA, TUCKER'S ISLAND

*This series of photographs was made by the grandnephew of Lighthouse Keeper Arthur H. T. Rider, who wrote in his official report: "Tower and dwelling except dining room and kitchen upset in the surf yesterday and was broken up and washed away by the sea."*

*"In the late 1940s, along the edge of the deep, new Beach Haven Inlet, flocks of seabirds stood at low tide on a long sand bar, all that was left of what had once been a five-mile island with trees, ponds, a lighthouse, a Coast Guard station, a school, two hotels and a proud little community. It had been New Jersey's first seashore resort. By 1952 even the birds had no place to stand. Tucker's Island had disappeared into history."*

— *John Bailey Lloyd, in*
Eighteen Miles of History on Long Beach Island

Black and white photographs by Paul Rider;
from *Eighteen Miles of History on Long Beach Island*

*c. 1920s*

## IN THE SURF, BEACH HAVEN

Black and white photograph:
Lloyd family collection

*late 1920s*

# FISHERMEN UNLOADING NETS AT BARNEGAT INLET

*Before Barnegat Inlet was enclosed by bulkheading and rock jetties, it was possible to bring a small boat up along the sandy shoreline. Here local fishermen transfer nets with the aid of a tractor. The original black and white photograph is by Paul Gill, an impressionist painter who was part of the Harvey Cedars "art colony" active in the 1920s and 1930s, and may have been made as a reference or study. At the time of his death in 1938, Gill was recognized as one of America's leading watercolorists.*

Black and white photograph by Paul Gill;
from an original print. Lloyd family collection

c. 1927

# FLORENCE HARTNETT DELIVERING MAIL ON MAYOR J.B. KINSEY'S HORSE, HARVEY CEDARS

*The north end of Harvey Cedars was known as High Point until the early 1930s, but the name was discontinued to avoid confusion with High Point in northwestern New Jersey. The earlier name survives today with the High Point Volunteer Fire Company.*

*"On the Island there were tiny little post office buildings in each community that were run mostly by women; they became well known as local characters, and whenever distribution was delayed they were always suspected of reading the postcards; it was a popular myth. The fact is they were efficient civil servants who handled an incredible volume of mail, especially in the summer months, and much of it to perfect strangers."*

*— John Bailey Lloyd, in Six Miles At Sea*

Black and white photograph:
Collection of Margaret Thomas Buchholz

*c. 1920s*

## HOLGATE, AFTER
## WORLD WAR I

*"The main road south from Beach Haven was widened in
the winter of 1921-1922, and campers began to roll in by the
hundreds. In the 1920s from May to October it was possible
to count as many as 50 or 60 tents on a weekend. It was
considered by many to be the perfect vacation. Plenty of World
War I surplus equipment was around, and people
were buying cars to carry it in."*

— *John Bailey Lloyd, in*
Two Centuries of History on Long Beach Island

Black and white photograph from
*Six Miles At Sea*

142

*c. 1930s*

# POUND FISHING SKIFF RETURNING TO SHORE, LONG BEACH ISLAND

*As many as a dozen boats from the five Island fisheries went out to the pounds in good weather and bad every day except Sunday in the 32-foot wide-beamed skiffs. "Nearly all of the pound boat crews and the other men who worked for the fisheries were Scandinavian, mostly Norwegian. There were a few Portuguese and many North Carolinians, who, it was said, had followed the trainloads of hickory poles up the coast to the pound nets. Nearly half of the men were single and lived over the packing sheds in barracks-type housing or dormitories with a galley, a mess room and usually a full-time cook. During the fishing season the men were roused at 4:30 a.m. for a huge breakfast of eggs, pancakes and mountains of sausages and pork chops."*

— *John Bailey Lloyd, in* Eighteen Miles of History on Long Beach Island

Black and white photograph from *Eighteen Miles of History on Long Beach Island*

145

# MOTORING TO LONG BEACH ISLAND ON S-40 IN THE PYGMY PINES OF THE PINE BARRENS

*"A new highway was rebuilt over and alongside the old in the late '40s — Routes 70 and 72. Traces of the old road remain along its southerly edge as an undulating track for dirt bikes. Today with all the traffic and the red lights it takes longer to drive down the shore than it did 50 years ago."*
— *John Bailey Lloyd in* Six Miles At Sea

Black and white photograph
from *Six Miles At Sea*

*1933*

# BARNEGAT LIGHTHOUSE
# AT RISK OF COLLAPSE

*Storms and powerful ebb tides nearly undercut the foundation of the lighthouse in the early 1930s. With the new Barnegat Lightship operating offshore, the federal Bureau of Lighthouses was willing to write off the obsolete tower. But local residents rallied to save it, at first dumping a ring of old cars and trucks around the base. Soon, the state awarded a contract to build a steel and concrete "petticoat" around the base. Completed in 1934, it remains in place today.*

Black and white photograph from
*Six Miles At Sea*

*c. 1930*

# BEACH HAVEN
# LIFEGUARDS

*The Island's first official beach patrol was established in 1927, through the efforts of Emily Lloyd Wilson. She ran swimming and lifesaving lessons for every child in Beach Haven and set up a fully equipped Red Cross emergency station on the boardwalk at Coral Street between the Baldwin and Engleside hotels. Prior to the borough-managed patrol, lifesaving was handled by the two big hotels, whose lifeguards were called "beach masters."*

Black and white photograph:
Roper, from an original print: Lloyd family collection

*c. 1920s*

## STOPPING FOR
## A PHOTOGRAPH,
## OLD CAUSEWAY

*"The water came right under the car. I used to get down on
the floor in the back seat on my knees and huddle down
there until we got across the long span. There were
always loose planks that would come up and the next
thing you know you'd have a flat tire from a nail."*
— *Becky Keil Tarditi, in* Island Album

Black and white photograph from
*Six Miles At Sea*

*1931*

## COAST GUARD DESTROYING RUMRUNNER'S CARGO, OFFSHORE BEACH HAVEN

*During Prohibition, smuggling was often a three-ship process, with fast motor launches that ferried cargo from "rum ships" 12 miles offshore to the nearest inlet. Locals in a big garvey would retrieve and hide the cache in a load of clams, oysters, or fish, and typically transfer it to a truck on its way to New York. Alcohol ended up in local speakeasies as well — including the Baldwin Hotel, Acme Hotel, Waverly Hotel (today's Hudson House), Wida's, and gun and yacht clubs.*

Black and white photograph from
*Six Miles At Sea*

*c. 1930*

## POUND FISHERMEN,
## LONG BEACH ISLAND

*"There was not a puny man among those pound fishermen.
They were all muscle and brawn, well over six feet tall and
most of them weighed over 200 pounds. They had terrific
appetites. They would get up about four in the morning and
each man would have about eight cups of coffee and a loaf
of bread apiece. After the fish were brought in the men went
to the cookhouse on 76th Street for breakfast. Each man ate
eight eggs, half a slice of ham, eight or ten more cups of coffee
and another loaf of bread. I remember this so well because
one of my jobs was to help out in the cookhouse."*

—— *Carlyle Stephen in* Island Album

Black and white photograph: Charles Edgar Nash,
from *Island Album*

# DUESENBERG STUCK
# IN THE SAND,
# LONG BEACH ISLAND

*The appeal of driving on the beach has been with drivers since the earliest years of the automobile, along with the challenges.*

Black and white photograph:
Lloyd family collection

*c. 1930*

## LIFEGUARDS,
## BEACH HAVEN

*The Beach Haven boardwalk can be
seen behind the lifeguard chair. Guard George Lee is standing;
his mother managed the Baldwin Hotel bathhouses.*

Black and white photograph:
Collection of the New Jersey Maritime Museum

*c. 1930*

## POT FISHERMEN CLEANING THEIR LOBSTER POTS, BARNEGAT CITY

*At the end of the season, fishermen would clean and re-tar their pots before storing them in the bait-up shacks at the Independent Docks. Each pot might catch not only lobster, but also sea bass or mackerel.*

Black and white photograph, from an original print:
Lloyd family collection

*c. 1930*

## SHOES AND SOCKS
## ON THE BEACH

Black and white photograph from
*Two Centuries of History on Long Beach Island*

*c. 1930s*

## POUND FISHING,
## LONG BEACH ISLAND

*Pound nets were set up with 30 to 40 poles, in about 36 feet of water two to three miles offshore. Fish were retrieved from the pounds each morning. Lucky observers on the beach might be tossed a sea bass or bonito, but most of the catch was sent to fish markets in New York or Philadelphia. Fishermen loaded 50-pound baskets for the Island's five fisheries which then packed the fish into barrels with ice for shipment by the railroad, and in later years by truck. The 1944 hurricane devastated the fishery's nets and poles, costs increased, and fish populations declined after World War II. The Crest Fishery was the last to operate on the Island, going out of business in 1956.*

Black and white photograph from
*Eighteen Miles of History on Long Beach Island*

*c. 1936*

## BRANT BEACH

*"Captain Storey talking to Joseph Moran,*
*Bayview Ave., Brant Beach."*

*— handwritten note on back of the photograph.*

Black and white photograph,
from an original print: Lloyd family collection

*c. 1930s*

## OLD CAUSEWAY, CEDAR BONNET ISLAND

*On the causeway just west of the drawbridge, looking toward the mainland, two bars offered those departing or arriving on the Island a drink and a meal. They also doubled as bait and tackle shops. Charlie Fackler's bar on the north side was sold to Otto Schmidt in 1952 and became the Dutchman's Brauhaus in 1965. Van's, on the south side, was torn down to make way for construction of the 1956 causeway.*

Black and white photograph from
*Six Miles at Sea*

*July 1936*

# LITTLE EGG HARBOR
# YACHT CLUB, BEACH HAVEN

*Sam Collum drove his new Pierce-Arrow over the yacht club bulkhead. The small boats moored at the dock are racing sneakboxes.*

Black and white photograph from
*Island Album*

*August 1936*

## HINDENBURG OVER
## BEACH HAVEN

*"From 1929 until 1937, the great trans-Atlantic zeppelins passed over Long Beach Island on their way to and from the Naval Air Station at Lakehurst.... Here the Hindenburg is heading south over Gifford's Garage in Beach Haven, in August of 1936. The airship had just left Lakehurst, and would make its turn out into the Atlantic from Atlantic City, in a tradition established by the Graf Zeppelin in 1929.... Not until 1939 were there any commercial airplanes in service designed to carry passengers across the Atlantic, and they had to refuel in Newfoundland or Bermuda."*

— *John Bailey Lloyd, in* Two Centuries of History on Long Beach Island

Black and white photograph from
*Two Centuries of History on Long Beach Island*

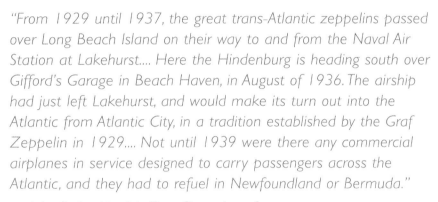

*c. 1930s*

## CEDAR RUN DOCK ROAD

*At the end of this winding road through the marsh to the bay, Bertram Cranmer offered fishing charters, rowboats, and tackle along with Stanley Conklin's place across the road. By the 1950s, both operated as commercial clam houses, and clams we so plentiful the Campbell Soup Company sent refrigerated trucks weekly to purchase them for soup.*

Black and white photograph:
Down The Shore Publishing collection

177

*1938*

## BEACH HAVEN

*Flood tide at Southwick's Boat Basin.*

Black and white photograph by Bill Kane:
Lloyd family collection

*late 1930s*

## BEACH HAVEN
## BEACH PATROL

*Behind the guards is Henry's Pavilion on the boardwalk at 2nd Street. Destroyed in the March 1962 storm, the building included changing rooms and a community outside shower; customers could play pinball or get hot dogs, hamburgers, or a favorite — waffles with ice cream.*

Black and white photograph, from an original print:
Lloyd family collection

*1939*

## DRIVING PAST REMAINS
## OF AN OLD SHIPWRECK,
## BEACH HAVEN TERRACE

*Meyers Haines, Thelma Bradford Chapman and*
*George Parker Jr. catch a ride in a Ford Model A*
*beach buggy near the skeleton of a wrecked ship.*

Black and white photograph from
*Island Album*

*Late 1930s*

## BEACH HAVEN
## BOARDWALK

*"The 1917 boardwalk shall always be
associated with the Beach Haven of the
years between the two world wars... an era
that came to an abrupt end with Pearl Harbor."*
— *John Bailey Lloyd in* Eighteen Miles of History
on Long Beach Island

Black and white photograph:
Lloyd family collection

*1940*

## REYNOLD THOMAS' DREDGE IN FOR REPAIRS, HARVEY CEDARS

*"My father, Reynold Thomas, bought a dredge in the mid-'30s, after an unsuccessful stint as a fisherman. His first customers were mostly wealthy summer people who owned an ocean-to-bay tract and wanted the bayside filled."*
— *Margaret Thomas Buchholz in* Island Album

Black and white photograph:
Collection of Margaret Thomas Buchholz

# BARNEGAT LIGHTHOUSE
# AND TOWER FOR
# JETTY CONSTRUCTION

*Barnegat Inlet was migrating south, threatening navigation and the lighthouse, and construction of a jetty on the north side of the inlet was finally authorized by the War Department in Washington. Two towers, anchored on the Island Beach and Barnegat City sides, were constructed, and huge jetty rocks, delivered by truck to the north end of the Island, were carried across the inlet in leather buckets on cables.*

Black and white photograph:
Collection of Margaret Thomas Buchholz

*c. 1940s*

## TUECKMANTEL FAMILY AT THE ACME HOTEL BAR, BEACH HAVEN

*Captain John Cranmer opened the Acme on Dock Road in 1904 and expanded it in 1913 as a popular hunting and fishing gathering place.*

*"Prohibition became the law of the land from 1919 until 1933. Nowhere was it more disregarded than at Beach Haven, where the rum fleet was only twelve miles off the coast and any young bayman with a boat was willing and able to get cases of whiskey in burlap bags from the drop-off points at the Beach Haven Inlet. In 1925, Cranmer sold his place to Gustave Tueckmantel. Illegal booze was brought into the Acme, but not through the famous trap door in the floor. That wasn't necessary, and no boat could even get under the hotel at any tide. But it was a good story, and celebrities flocked there even when Prohibition was long over. They liked the Tueckmantels and the whole atmosphere."*
— *John Bailey Lloyd, in*
Eighteen Miles of History on Long Beach Island

Black and white photograph from
*Six Miles at Sea*

# INLET INN AFTER THE GREAT ATLANTIC STORM, HOLGATE

*The Inlet Inn, operated by William DeFreitas, evolved from a small hunting and fishing club offering beer and whiskey during Prohibition to a charming, character-filled neighborhood bar at the end of the Island. The building, along with 121 other homes in Holgate, was destroyed in the 1944 hurricane, and DeFreitas moved his tavern business north to Beach Haven Crest. His new namesake bar (years later: Kubel's Too) was a success, but he would always regale his customers with stories of the wonderful old days at the Inlet Inn.*

Black and white photograph from
*Six Miles At Sea*

*September 1944*

## HOMES DESTROYED BY THE HURRICANE, SHIP BOTTOM

Black and white photograph by New Jersey State Police;
from *Great Storms of the Jersey Shore*

*September 1944*

## AFTERMATH OF THE GREAT ATLANTIC HURRICANE, HOLGATE

*"Mrs. John Whitten, age 65 ... who lost her recently purchased home when storm swept it off of the foundation and into bay, at Holgate. Mrs. Whitten lost everything but sweater and bag she took with her when she went to the mainland before the storm. She is shown standing at what was once a bus stop along Ocean Blvd."*
— *from the New Jersey State Police files*

Black and white photograph
by New Jersey State Police;
from *Great Storms of the Jersey Shore*

*September 1944*

## POLICE CAR MIRED IN SAND AFTER THE HURRICANE, BRIGHTON BEACH

Black and white photograph: from Jane Smith;
in *Great Storms of the Jersey Shore*

*1944*

## DEBRIS IN THE AFTERMATH OF THE GREAT ATLANTIC HURRICANE, HOLGATE

Black and white photograph from an original print:
Lloyd family collection

## 1944

# AFTERMATH OF THE GREAT ATLANTIC HURRICANE, HOLGATE

*The hurricane of September 14, 1944 devastated all of Long Beach Island, but Holgate was especially hard hit. Four elderly women drowned there, and a two-year-old girl was lost. Of 121 houses in Holgate only 19 were still standing after the storm.*

Black and white photograph from an original print:. Lloyd family collection

*1944*

## ASSESSING THE DAMAGE
## AFTER THE HURRICANE

*The Great Atlantic Hurricane of September 14
deposited a house on the road along the
Harvey Cedars - North Beach line.*

Black and white photograph by Bill Kane;
from *Great Storms of the Jersey Shore*

*1945*

## HARVEY CEDARS

*Long Beach Island was not prepared for the Great Atlantic Hurricane of September 14, 1944. For some it was life or death as homes and other structures were torn apart in the storm surge. Six months later, in the spring of 1945, Carolyn Wilcox stands oceanside at 78th Street in Harvey Cedars where she and her family were caught in the surging tide as they tried to make it to safety at the general store.*

Black and white photograph
from *Long Beach Island Chronicles*

c. *1940s*

# HEADING TOWARD MANAHAWKIN, U.S. ROUTE 9

*Until the Garden State Parkway*
*was built in 1954, Route 9 was the*
*two-lane highway for travelers from*
*New York and North Jersey. The Long*
*Beach Island signs by Tooker Sign*
*Co. of Tuckerton were landmarks as*
*drivers approached from both the*
*north and south.*

Black and white photograph
from *Six Miles At Sea*

*c. 1948*

## THE *LUCY EVELYN,* BEACH HAVEN

*When the Lucy Evelyn was towed from New England to Beach
Haven in June 1948 she was stranded in the bay near Mordecai
Island through October until a northeaster-driven flood tide floated
the schooner into a final berth, a dredged basin at 9th Street.*

*"She was an attention getter. Few persons in the daily parade
of small pleasure boats using the channel to and from the inlet
had ever been this close to a big, ocean-going, wind ship. From the
waterline they viewed the dizzying height of her three masts of
Oregon pine, each over 100 feet tall. A graceful bowsprit added
yet another score of feet to the length of her hull. No ship
of her size had ever been this far up the bay."*

— *John Bailey Lloyd, in* Six Miles At Sea

Black and white photograph from
*Six Miles At Sea*

# POSING WITH A CATCH AT THE BEACH HAVEN YACHT CLUB

*From its origins in 1882 as an organization for professional captains of the big catboats who ferried passengers and freight across the bay, to a social, fishing and boating group, the Beach Haven Yacht Club is a legendary part of the Island's history. At the end of a summer's day the weighing station was the backdrop for many prize catches, especially during tuna and marlin tournaments. The club's building was sold and demolished to make way for condominiums in 1985.*

Black and white photograph:
collection of the New Jersey Maritime Museum

*1948*

## DUSTER NATIONAL CHAMPIONSHIP, BRANT BEACH YACHT CLUB

*The Duster was a popular sailboat on New Jersey waters in the mid-20th century; it was designed in 1933 and built in Riverton, N.J. The Brant Beach Yacht Club, as well as the Barnegat Light Yacht Club (in Harvey Cedars), had a fleet of Dusters.*

Black and white photograph:
Collection of Margaret Thomas Buchholz

# THE *LUCY EVELYN,*
# BEACH HAVEN

*Until she was destroyed in fire in 1972, the Lucy Evelyn was as much of an attraction on the south end of Long Beach Island as the lighthouse to the north. In 1948 Nat Ewer purchased the 160-foot, sloop-rigged cargo schooner, built in 1917, had her towed from New Bedford to Beach Haven, and created a gift shop and tourist attraction like no other. It was operated to replace The Sea Chest, his shop on the Beach Haven boardwalk, which was destroyed in the hurricane of 1944. On opening day, May 30, 1949, nearly 10,000 people visited the repurposed ship — crowds that rivaled the opening of the causeway in 1914. For 22 years, the graceful windjammer, landlocked at 9th Street, was an Island landmark.*

Black and white photograph:
Lloyd family collection

*c. 1950s*

# SPRAYING DDT,
# THE DUNES,
# LONG BEACH TOWNSHIP

*"Back in the 1950s and '60s on quiet summer evenings at the Shore, there was never a sound that excited children more than the hiss of the approaching DDT, or as it was called, the "Drop Dead Twice" truck. ...No mosquito would bite you for the rest of the evening. You could breathe it and even rub it into your hair. DDT was good for you and bad for bugs. Even the adults half believed this, sitting on their screened porches at cocktail hour. When the thick mist from the jeep enveloped them, they simply put a hand over their gin and tonics, and someone might put a napkin over the dip, until the air was clear again."*

— John Bailey Lloyd, *in* Two Centuries of History on Long Beach Island

Black and white photograph from
*Two Centuries of History on Long Beach Island*

*c. 1950*

## SINBAD, THE COAST GUARD MASCOT, BARNEGAT LIGHT

*Sinbad, the Coast Guard's most famous mascot, was always served a beer at Kubel's. After being adopted from a New York City dog pound, he came aboard the cutter U.S.S. Campbell in 1937 and served aboard the ship until 1948. He was transferred to less adventurous assignments at the Barnegat Light Coast Guard station, appeared in newspapers and a biography, and spent his final years in the company of locals or snoozing in the station's lookout tower. Sinbad died in 1951 and is buried near the station.*

Black and white photograph from
*The Long Beach Island Reader*

c. *1950s*

## OPENING THE CAUSEWAY DRAWBRIDGE FOR BOAT TRAFFIC

*"I, among tens of thousands of others, had sat in the long line-ups of cars over the years. I had also approached the drawbridge by boat and watched the traffic pile up in both directions and felt a twinge of guilt and pity — guilt for causing the jam and pity for the motorists. But I have always regretted that my children would never have the thrill of having the drawbridge raised just for them."*

— *Margaret Thomas Buchholz, in* Island Album

Black and white photograph from
*Island Album*

*c. 1950s*

## STORM TIDE,
## BEACH HAVEN BAYSIDE

*3rd Street, Beach Haven.*

Black and white photograph:
Lloyd family collection

# INDEPENDENT DOCK, BARNEGAT LIGHT

*The commercial dock, having expanded from its earlier days in this photograph, became known as Viking Village because of all the Scandanavian fishermen in Barnegat Light. The empty marshland in the distance would later become High Bar Harbor.*

*"We were shipping fish up to Dick Myers (Barnegat City Fishery), but he kept charging us more and more for the barrels, so we 22 Norwegian guys, we put our heads together. We went to a guy named Everett Jones. He had a lot of land along the bay there. So we asked him how much he wanted for a block of land; $3,000, he said. Well, we went to the bank and we got a note that was that long — for 22 to sign. We paid Jones off and chipped in ten bucks each to a fund to get started. They tore up the bridge over to the mainland and we got the planking for 25 cents each. We had to take them away ourselves; we had one gang loading and one unloading. Ashbrook Cranmer over in Mayetta, he done roadwork and so he said, 'I'm going to help you pump the pump.' ...So he lent us the pump and we put the pilings down. We became carpenters; we built the whole dock in the winter of 1926-27, 120-feet long."*

— *Chris Halversen in* Island Album

Black and white photograph:
Collection of Margaret Thomas Buchholz

*1952*

## TIDAL FLOODING, BEACH HAVEN

*Frequent northeasters in the early 1950s flooded the
Island with storm-driven tides. In Beach Haven, Bay Avenue is
temporarily reclaimed by the bay. This section of Long Beach
Boulevard was so named because in the founding of the resort
town it was the westernmost street, nearest the bay.*

Black and white photograph:
Collection of Margaret Thomas Buchholz

*1954*

# ANTLERS BAR,
# BEACH HAVEN

*"The Antlers was a bar for conversation and game playing. There was a juke box in the front room on the Dock Road side. You got six songs for a quarter, but it was never loud enough to drown out the constant thunk of darts and slamming of the men's room door. The great attraction of the place was that it was here that all the boys on the Island would gather on summer nights to meet the girls. The classic conversation opener was, "Where do you go to school? Do you know so and so?" The college students of the early '50s were a very underpopulated generation who quite unselfconsciously thought of themselves as boys and girls. The war babies were toddlers, and it really was possible to know someone in every eastern college. Both sexes went barefoot to the bars at night. In the decades of the '50s and most of the '60s no young person ever wore shoes at the Shore anywhere but to the movies, where they were required or you didn't get in."*
— *John Bailey Lloyd, in* Eighteen Miles of History on Long Beach Island.

Black and white photograph from
*Island Album*

231

# NAVY AIRSHIP,
# LONG BEACH ISLAND

*"Blimps" from the Naval Air Station in Lakehurst were a common sight off the beach during World War II, patrolling for German submarines. They were frequently spotted on maneuvers tracking Soviet submarines into the early 1960s.*

*"From the third floor of Conrad Brothers Lumber Company in Ship Bottom I could watch the convoys, preceded by blimps, going by — mostly oil tankers going from the Gulf of Mexico to the Northeast and back. They beefed up the Coast Guard patrol with 24-hour surveillance of the beach. At the very beginning of the war, before the blackout, German subs could see the ships outlined against the lights of Atlantic City, and many tankers were sunk."*

— *Tom Oakley, in* Island Album

Black and white photograph from
*Six Miles At Sea*

*1954*

## BIG TUNA,
## CREST FISHERY

*The Beachcomber newspaper's "Prize Catch of the Week" was this monster tuna brought in to the Crest Fishery. Tonnes Bohn, owner of the fishery, is above the tuna, fourth from the right. Crest was the last pound fishery operating on the Island, hanging on with a consortium of investors as others went out of business, but it, too, ceased all pound fishing in 1956.*

Black and white photograph:
Collection of Margaret Thomas Buchholz

*1953*

# FLOODING FROM A
# NORTHEASTER, BEACH HAVEN

*Milton Britz, owner of Britz's Bar, at the corner of
Centre Street and Bay Avenue, stands in the
flood tide from a northeaster November 7, 1953.*

Black and white photograph from
*Great Storms of the Jersey Shore*

*1956*

## ORIGINAL CAUSEWAY AND CONSTRUCTION OF THE NEW BRIDGE, LOOKING EAST

*"... In 1956 the old causeway was dwarfed by huge concrete supports of a new steel bridge being built 100 feet to the south. Three years later, the old causeway, so familiar to all, was gone. The wooden bridges were removed, and all that remains of the old span are parts of the roadway on Cedar Bonnet Island and on the mainland in Hilliard (Mud City) as an extension of East Bay Avenue."*

— John Bailey Lloyd in
Eighteen Miles of History on Long Beach Island

Black and white photograph:
Lloyd family collection

*1954*

# ANTICS AT THE ANTLERS BAR,
# BEACH HAVEN

*"The Antlers had been abandoned for years, but it is remembered by a whole generation with great affection and nostalgia. Early in the century — when Dock Road was still a canal — it was a hunting and fishing club for a splinter group of the Elks Lodge in Philadelphia and became a speakeasy during the Prohibition era. After 1933 it became a public bar, run by Bill Van Kirk, and later Larry Johnson.... Every horizontal space, every window sill, every shelf on a summer night seemed to be covered with partially filled or empty beer glasses. Hanging high on the walls all around both rooms, half hidden in the haze of cigarette smoke, was a moth-eaten collection of stuffed deer and elk heads, relics of the bar's early years as a hunting club. All bars attract characters, and there was a grizzled old-timer in a yachting cap named Captain Vince, a regular patron who, about once or twice a summer, carrying a chair to stand on, went around the room with an empty pail offering each of the deer heads a drink."*

— *John Bailey Lloyd, in* Eighteen Miles of History on Long Beach Island

Black and white photograph:
Lloyd family collection

*1956*

# OLD CAUSEWAY AND CONSTRUCTION OF THE NEW BRIDGE, LOOKING WEST

*"When you were leaving the Island on the old causeway during a hurricane, you drove over the completely flooded flat roadway; it looked as though you were about to drive over water with nothing under it! The new bridge is too efficient, the sense of adventure is gone with such security. One of the great things about the Island was its wildness."*
— *Paula Kelly Muller, in* Island Album

Black and white photograph from
*Eighteen Miles of History on Long Beach Island*

# ACME HOTEL, DOCK ROAD, BEACH HAVEN

*Bird and Betty Clutter, new owners of the bar, standing on the porch, welcomed a younger generation in the 1960s and early '70s. But from 1925 through the '50s the Acme had been "the exclusive territory of the sport-fishing crowd and the town's native population. College students were as welcome here as greenhead flies," author John Bailey Lloyd wrote. The Acme opened for business in 1904 and was expanded in 1913, before Mud Hen Creek, the canal along Dock Road that was the original entrance to Beach Haven, was filled in.*

Black and white photograph from
*Six Miles At Sea*

*early 1960s*

## LONGBOARDS
## AND LEGENDS

*Ron DiMenna and Rev. Earl Comfort (first and second from left), along with John Spodafora, helped introduce surfing to Long Beach Island by making and selling boards. Ron Jon Surf Shop grew out of their first trailer load of boards, which they sold in Ship Bottom.*

Black and white photograph:
Collection of Margaret Thomas Buchholz

# BALDWIN HOTEL FIRE, BEACH HAVEN

*"Near midnight on September 24, 1960, with the hotel deserted, a blaze began again in the east wing and, driven by gale-force winds off the sea, resulted in the most spectacular fire ever seen on the Jersey coast. Twenty fire companies showed up, some from as far south as Pleasantville and as far north as Toms River. The hotel was destroyed. The vacant lot was sold the following spring to Holy Innocents' Episcopal Church of Beach Haven, and it is now occupied by a church, parish house and brick-walled memorial garden."*

— *John Bailey Lloyd, in*
Eighteen Miles of History on Long Beach Island

Black and white photograph from
*Eighteen Miles of History on Long Beach Island*

*March 1962*

## AFTERMATH OF THE GREAT ATLANTIC STORM, HARVEY CEDARS

*The legendary three-day northeaster cut Long Beach Island into five islands; an active inlet at 79th Street in Harvey Cedars exchanged tides between bay and ocean for days. Seven Islanders died in the storm, including three officials who drowned when their truck submerged in Holgate. Two hundred seventy homes were destroyed and 180 sustained major damage. Within a year the state passed construction legislation requiring all new homes to be built on pilings.*

Black and white photograph "from Bert Stratton's scrapbook," Beach Haven Library

*March 1962*

# AFTERMATH OF THE GREAT ATLANTIC STORM, BEACH HAVEN

*The beach pavilion in the surf is at 5th Street.*

*"It had been, everybody agreed, some storm. It did more damage to the Jersey coast than any storm before.... Newspapers wore out adjectives trying to describe it. Finally the U.S. Weather Bureau gave it a name.... It became The Great Atlantic Storm. 'The magnitude of the storm, it seemed to us, made it necessary to give it a classification, an official name,' said Charles Knudsen, a New Jerseyan who headed the bureau's headquarters in New York."*

*— from* Great Storms of the Jersey Shore

Black and white photograph by Abe Josephson:
Lloyd family collection

## March 1962

# BEACHED DESTROYER
# *U.S.S. MONSSON, HOLGATE*

*A veteran of intense action in the war in the Pacific, the decommissioned warship was being towed to join the mothball fleet at the Philadelphia Navy Yard when the towline snapped in the midst of the three-day northeaster. The 376-foot long destroyer was driven ashore and beached on March 6 just south of the end of Long Beach Boulevard. It was six weeks later, April 19, before the 2,000-ton ship was re-floated and completed her journey, ultimately sold for scrap.*

Black and white photograph:
Lloyd family collection

*1967*

# MANAHAWKIN DRIVE-IN

Built just east of the old Manahawkin Airport, drivers heading toward Long Beach Island could get a free show (without sound) by parking on the shoulder of Route 72.

Black and white photograph from
*Stafford Chronicles: A History of Manahawkin, New Jersey*

*c. 1960s*

## GUARDED BEACH,
## BARNEGAT LIGHT

*This section of the borough's beach is now protected for
globally threatened, and New Jersey endangered,
piping plovers during the nesting season.*

Black and white photograph from
*Island Album*

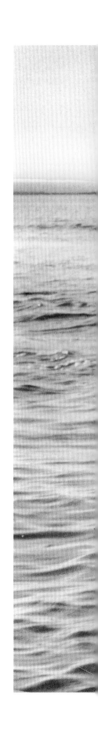

*c. 1970*

## CAUGHT IN THE
## INCOMING TIDE,
## HOLGATE

Black and white photograph:
Collection of Margaret Thomas Buchholz

*1970*

# CONTEMPORARY ARCHITECTURE, LOVELADIES

*One of the last undeveloped areas of Long Beach Island, the stretch of ocean-to-bay tracts from Harvey Cedars to Barnegat Light was an exciting blank slate for creative, modernist architects from the 1950s through the 1970s. The area was named by the U.S. Life-Saving Service when a local name was chosen for a station in 1871. Thomas Lovelady had hunted on the namesake Lovelady's Island, a small island in the bay lost to erosion in the 1920s.*

Black and white photograph: Stephen Hill;
Collection of Margaret Thomas Buchholz

*early 1970s*

## BEACH BUDDIES,
## SURF CITY

Black and white photograph by
Emilio J. Labrador: Collection of Margaret Thomas Buchholz

*c. 1970s*

## SURF FISHERMEN,
## LONG BEACH ISLAND

Black and white photograph:
Collection of Margaret Thomas Buchholz

*c. 1978*

## SKELETON OF A GARVEY, NORTH BEACH

*On the Harvey Cedars edge of North Beach, a small tidal creek ran toward Barnegat Bay, with a pair of abandoned boats claiming the marshland as a final resting place. This natural bayfront was one of the last undeveloped parcels on the Island and is now dotted with houses on filled salt marsh.*

Black and white photograph by Ray Fisk, hand-colored with Marshall's Photo Oils for the 1987 *Down The Shore Calendar.*

*c. 1980*

## COMMERCIAL FISHING BOATS IN WINTER, BARNEGAT LIGHT

Black and white photograph by Ray Fisk, hand-colored with
Marshall's Photo Oils for the 1987 *Down The Shore Calendar*

*1980*

## POLLY'S DOCK,
## BEACH HAVEN

Photograph by Ray Fisk,
hand-colored with Marshall's Photo Oils,
as published in the 1987 *Down The Shore Calendar.*

# THE SHACK
# ON THE CAUSEWAY

*The legendary Shack greeted everyone as they crossed over the bridge onto Cedar Bonnet Island. In its final decades, until Superstorm Sandy washed it away, the shack seemed as iconic as Barnegat Lighthouse. Nearly everyone felt possessive of it. Built around 1920, it was used by a group of families as a gunning and fishing club and known as the "Happy Days Lodge." It was last rented by free spirits in the late 1970s who relished a simple lifestyle as close to nature as you could get.*

Black and white photograph by Ray Fisk for *New Jersey Outdoors Magazine,* hand-colored with Marshall's Photo Oils.

## c. 1920s
## HOLGATE

*Camping in the Holgate dunes was popular in the early 1900s, and Horner, who as a young man had worked for Thomas Bond, ran a primitive campground.*

Black and white photograph:
Lloyd family collection

# AFTERWORD
*The back story.*

Thirty-five years ago we published the third Down The Shore Calendar, for 1987, with hand-colored black and white contemporary photographs. The prints were made on fiber paper and, using Marshall's Photo Oil paints, were tinted using the same method as hand-colored photographs from the early 20th century. We took creative liberties with the colors on some — it was fun — but, commercially, that year's calendar was a flop. We'll chalk it up as a passionate art project.

The hand-coloring in this book is more focused. It's about sharing local history by giving new life to old photographs. Instead of photo oils, in this digital age, the new work was done on a computer. But it's honest coloring, done — tediously but lovingly — by hand and using the intuitive, visual, right side of the human brain. The artist must make countless tiny decisions about everything from the color of the marsh grass (subtle shifts in every season), or water and sky, to buildings, boats, and the hue of skin.

In recent years, we've come to expect a simple click can change anything — that a magic digital filter can instantly alter the look, feel, and mood of an image. Apps and algorithms are already arriving that will make historic black and white photos "colorized." No doubt resulting images will have appeal. But what will be missing will be the close examination of details in

BEACH HAVEN, CENTRE STREET BEACH c. 1981:
*This black and white print was traditionally hand-colored with photo oils for the third* Down The Shore Calendar, *but never used.*

BEFORE AND AFTER: *This original 1944 hurricane photograph just cried out for color — the man's storm-wrecked home, all the destruction and belongings on the ground in front of him — yet he seems thrilled about the "Beach Buggy Service" sign. You can see how the photo was lightened a bit so the color would "shine." And does his reflection in the door window get lost in back and white?*

the original print, and the human understanding (and sensing) about what shade of color the tiniest feature should have. (Is this metal rust-colored, or shiny, or grey? It helps to be human, to live at the Shore, and understand time and proximity to salt water on objects like metal.) For us, there is satisfaction in knowing the work in this book was done with craftsman-like effort.

We gave this book the subtitle "Long Beach Island's Historical Photographs Reimagined." Reimagined refers to the fact that, in most cases, we don't know precisely the color of particular clothing, boats, or houses. The people who could tell us are no longer with us. There are few color references, although some written documents describe original colors. (This is the case with some details of the Little Egg Harbor Lighthouse on Tucker's Island, thanks to government records.) In any event, color decisions involve a lot of thinking and we may occasionally get it wrong, but in most cases there is a conscious awareness to get it right. (A few of the images in this book are from that 1987 calendar project, and on those you may notice a different approach to coloring; for example, the Polly's Dock image on page 272.)

We've strived for fidelity to history and to the photographs. If there were "flaws" in the original prints — due to aging, stains, dark and light areas, fading, or darkening, these issues were approached with a delicate touch. In the case of very bad quality prints, editing and adjusting the black and white scans was necessary to even attempt coloring the image. We may have digitally "repaired" a tear in a brittle old print, or cleaned up smudges, but did not want to retouch the images in any way that altered the historical integrity. In fact, we believe some imperfections and flaws need to remain

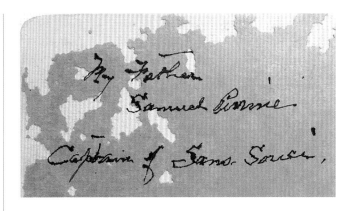

CLUES AND CONTEXT: *Working with original historic prints is especially rewarding when the past is revealed in notations made on the back over a century ago.*

for authenticity's sake, to add an honesty to the material.

Interestingly, some of the original prints were already "enhanced" at the time by airbrush artists. These craftsmen, usually found in newspaper and magazine art departments or photography studios, would work on the gelatin-silver prints "noodling" a picture, perhaps adding definition or lightening or darkening areas, or painting clouds in a plain sky. The craft was like an analog version of Photoshop. If we found these treatments in the original prints, we left them in place as artifacts from another time. (An example of this can be found on page 36 — in the original 1890s print of the *Owl*, the sky and water are noticably airbrushed.)

We've "lived" with these images, immersed ourselves in them. After almost four decades of handling and examining historic photos of Long Beach Island and the Shore, the thrill of discovering and working with original prints is still there.

1924
## BEACH HAVEN

Black and white photograph from an original print: Lloyd family collection

*1944*

## LONG BEACH ISLAND BOARD OF TRADE, CAUSEWAY, SHIP BOTTOM

*Founded when the first causeway was built in 1914, the organization eventually became the Chamber of Commerce. Long before Chowderfest, one of the main events sponsored was a "Miss Magic Long Beach Island" beauty contest, beginning in 1957. Young women submitted photographs from which a weekly winner was chosen, and a final Miss Magic was crowned at a pageant held at the end of summer.*

Black and white photograph from *Island Album*

# SELECTED BIBLIOGRAPHY

*Long Beach Island authors and Long Beach Island books.*

**John Bailey Lloyd's** trilogy of LBI pictorial histories not only captures the historical details, but also evoke the spirit of earlier generations. The Island's three foundational books are:
- *Eighteen Miles of History on Long Beach Island*
- *Six Miles At Sea: A Pictorial History of Long Beach Island*
- *Two Centuries of History on Long Beach Island*

John also provided fascinating local context in his introduction to a reissue of the 1906 Victorian novel *The Tides of Barnegat*, by F. Hopkinson Smith, and was the centerpiece of three LBI Historical Videos: *Barnegat Lighthouse and Barnegat City; Tuckers Island;* and *Six Miles At Sea.*

**Margaret Thomas "Poochy" Buchholz,** long-time editor of *The Beachcomber,* a passionate researcher, has authored or edited seven books about LBI and the Shore:
- *Island Album: Photographs & Memories of Long Beach Island* — an oversize collection of photographs and oral history.
- *The Long Beach Island Reader* — a delightful anthology for the Island.
- *Long Beach Island Chronicles* — a curated selection of great writing from LBI publications.
- *New Jersey Shipwrecks: 350 Years in the Graveyard of the Atlantic* — a large-format history of the most significant wrecks along our shore.
- *Shore Chronicles: Diaries and Travelers' Tales from the Jersey Shore 1764-1955* — "As fresh as a sea breeze," said *Library Journal.*
- *Josephine: From Washington Working Girl to Fisherman's Wife*

— The true story of a 20th century woman ahead of her time who made LBI home.
- *Fisherman's Wife* — Beautifully illustrated by **Julie Goldstein**, a moving essay of love and adversity on LBI.

*Great Storms of the Jersey Shore*, by **Larry Savadove** and **Margaret Thomas Buchholz**, updated and expanded in a 2nd Edition by Scott Mazzella — "one of the best documented compendiums" of coastal storms, said *The New York Times*. In gripping stories and dramatic pictures this national award-winning book provides historical context for all storms until Sandy.

*Surviving Sandy: Long Beach Island and the Greatest Storm of the Jersey Shore*, by **Scott Mazzella**, documents the remarkable experience and resilience of the LBI community in the worst storm in generations.

*Four Seasons At the Shore* — This large-format art hardcover with hundreds of photographs and scores of contributors is heavily weighted toward LBI. Island writers including **Larry Savadove, Sandy Gingras, and Margaret Thomas Buchholz** contribute evocative seasonal essays.

The traditional Southern Ocean County lifestyle, rarely experienced by visitors these days, is shared in *The Bayman: A Life on Barnegat Bay,* by **Merce Ridgway.**

*Closed Sea: From Manasquan to the Mullica, A History of Barnegat Bay*, by **Kent Mountford** — the history, the environment, and the culture of the region.

*Jersey Shore Impressionists: The Fascination of Sun and Sea 1880-1940*, by **Roy Pedersen** — the groundbreaking art history of the Shore, which includes the "art colony" at Harvey Cedars.

*The Oyster Singer* — columnist and author **Larry Savadove's** evocative novel explores authentic local characters escaping the contemporary world on a changing LBI.

*Tales From An Endless Summer* — **Bruce Novotny's** lyrical coming-of-age surfing novel, set on the Island in a 1980s summer, continues to ring true.

Author and poet **Sandy Gingras'** first book, *How To Live on An Island,* was followed by *How To Live At the Beach, Reasons To Be Happy at the Beach,* and *At the Beach House: A Guest Book*, all inspired by LBI, and many other titles sold nationally. Her latest book, *I Love You Long Beach Island,* conceived during Superstorm Sandy, celebrates the fragility, beauty, and strength of this Island.

**Gretchen Coyle** and **Deb Whitcraft's** *Tucker's Island* explores in pictures and text the lost resort at the southern tip of LBI. Their large-format book *Inferno At Sea,* about the *Morro Castle* disaster at Asbury Park, is a companion book to the largest collection of *Morro Castle* items, at the New Jersey Maritime Museum in Beach Haven.

**Corinne G. Ruff's** *Island Child: Life Lessons From the Shore,* illustrated by Lisa Benjamin, shares residents' and visitors' delights and philosophy inspired by LBI.

*Stafford Chronicles* (by the staff of *The SandPaper*) profiles many of the figures whose lives left a mark on LBI and explores the shared history of mainland and Island.

Fascinating historical accounts from LBI, the Shore, and the entire state can be found in *New Jersey In History: Fighting to be Heard,* by **Thomas Farner**.

*Too Many Summers*, by **L. Ganss,** a collection of three decades of LBI-centric cartoons from *The SandPaper*, captures the ironies and humor of this summer resort in all seasons.

*1980*

## TREADING FOR CLAMS, MANAHAWKIN BAY

*A view from the Causeway.*

Black and white photograph by Ray Fisk,
hand-colored with Marshall's Photo Oils,
as published in the 1987 *Down The Shore Calendar*

# ACKNOWLEDGMENTS

We started this project casually, hand-coloring images in our archives from books we've published since 1986. Soon we realized we needed to revisit the original photographs, and knew there was more we should consider.

Without the following people, the rich historical record of Long Beach Island would be greatly diminished. We're grateful for access to their photographs, for their time, and for their good memory and knowledge as we checked dates, locations, and context.

We're indebted to **Jeanette Lloyd** for sharing her entire collection — and her deep knowledge of Island history. She shared background, historical details, and great local stories. A dedicated preservationist, she is largely responsible for creating and saving Beach Haven's Historic District, a remarkable achievement. In her own way, she also carries on the legacy of the late **John Bailey Lloyd**, whose foundational trilogy of books about Long Beach Island history gave us an awareness of this Island's past. We spent weeks with her collection, hoping to locate the original prints we published in those books. Searching through boxes, files, and crates, we discovered more wonderful photos, which fortunately resulted in expanding the material in this book.

**Margaret Thomas Buchholz** generously shared her own collection of Island photographs, gathered as editor and publisher of *The Beachcomber* from the 1950s through the 1980s. A passionate researcher, she is the author or editor of many essential Long Beach Island (as well as Jersey Shore) historical books, and enthusiastically confirmed or corrected dates and locations.

**Ron Marr** of the Long Beach Island Historical Association Museum was key when it came to the detective work of finding details to help date photographs and identify locations. And he was more than generous with his time researching background, and locating photographs.

**Reilly P. Sharp** of the Barnegat Light Museum offers an amazing wealth of historical Island knowledge, especially about the north end and Barnegat Light. We thank him for sharing images from the collection he meticulously digitized. He was particularly helpful with detailed background, and in clarifying uncertain dates and locations.

**Deb Whitcraft** is founder of the New Jersey Maritime Museum in Beach Haven — an incredible resource of maritime history — and was kind enough to share images from her files. With **Gretchen Coyle**, she is also a regional history author, and they offered historical background, dates, and locations; we are grateful.

And thanks to **Anita Josephson** for diligent and expeditious proofreading.

At this point, in 2021, many of the photographs that appear in this book, and in our other titles, have been copied, shared, copied again, shared online, and added to multiple collections. The original photographer or source who should be credited may be lost to time. If known, the primary sources are noted.

For the historical record, an acknowledgment is due a few specific photographers and collections that have survived into the 21st century. We are fortunate to have the work of the following available.

Credit for many of the Island's historic photographs found today should go to Lynn Photo Service, which continued to operate into the 2000s despite the demise of film. Harold "Monk" Lynn was a commercial and portrait photographer who came to the Island in 1929 and began building a collection of scenic negatives. Carl "Van" Thulin, an employee and photographer, bought the business in 1962 and greatly expanded that documentation of the community. Lynn Photo's catalogued archive was privately sold after the shop closed. However many of the individual prints purchased in the store now circulate widely.

Bill Kane, who ran the Nor'easter store in Beach Haven Terrace, starting in the 1930s, was obsessive

about photographing his surroundings. He used a big Speed Graphic camera and sold his pictures on hand-processed postcards. His photographs of the 1944 hurricane are in the collection of the Long Beach Island Historical Association Museum, and most of his other negatives were purchased by Lynn Photo.

Most of the earliest Beach Haven beach activity photographs were made by Robert F. Engle on large format glass plate negatives. Son of the founder of the Engleside Hotel, he was a professionally trained photographer who worked with the leading travel lecturer of the day. His scenic, playful, and artfully posed photographs of what we might call "lifestyle" today are invaluable documents of the earliest days of Beach Haven.

c. 1980s

# THE KETCH, BEACH HAVEN

*Leslee Ganss'* childhood summers were spent on the beaches of Harvey Cedars, and she's been here year 'round since 1979. After graduating from the Philadelphia College of Art with a degree in Illustration, she joined the fledgling SandPaper in 1980 and was the Art Director until 1996. She left to design books for Down The Shore Publishing, but continues a three-decade run of weekly Artoons in the paper. Her own work appears in four books, and in Local Color she combines her painting skills with the storytelling of her illustration background to make the historic black and white photographs come alive.

*Ray Fisk* founded Down The Shore Publishing in Harvey Cedars in 1984 while working as a photojournalist for The New York Times, United Press International, and The Philadelphia Inquirer. Throughout the '80s he covered Atlantic City, the Jersey Shore from Sandy Hook to the backwaters of the Delaware Bay, and southern New Jersey. In 1977 he helped establish The SandPaper and worked there until 1983 as associate editor and photography editor.

*Down The Shore Publishing specializes in books, calendars, cards and videos about Long Beach Island and the Shore. If you enjoyed this book you may also be interested in our other titles, including the books referenced here. Visit our website:*

**down-the-shore.com**

*Or for a catalog just send us a request —*
info@down-the-shore.com
Down The Shore Publishing, Box 100, West Creek, NJ 08092